I'm So READY for LIFE

BOOK 2

I Want to be A Leader, too

JOSEPH WONG

Illustrated by Joy Wong

jeiokiart@gmail. com

ISBN
978-1-5437-4019-6 (sc)
978-1-5437-4020-2 (e)

Print information available on the last page.

To order additional copies of this book, contact
Toll Free 800 101 2657 (Singapore)
Toll Free 1 800 81 7340 (Malaysia)
www.partridgepublishing.com/singapore
orders.singapore@partridgepublishing.com

04/20/2018

PARTRIDGE

Contents

A few words about this book

My message to kids

Why did I write this book? One day, you will finish school and look for a job. That can be scary when you do not know enough about how the world works and how adults think and behave. This book contains useful tips to prepare you to work with adults in the real world.

Why should you read this book? Well, I worked 36 years in an international bank. That makes me very old, right? Yeah...well, I can't do anything about my age but I certainly can share my 36-year experience with you - the mistakes I made, the lessons I learned and the things that made me succeed in my job. I put all these lessons into this book so that you will learn to avoid making those same mistakes.

So while this book prepares you for the future, you have to study hard in the meantime and make your parents proud of you, okay? Enjoy this book and you can write to me if you have any questions. I hope that by the time you finish school, you can confidently say, "I am so ready for life!".

My message to parents

Thank you for buying this book for your child. As a parent myself, I am mindful that our children face a future that's not as predictable as we are used to. I believe that our children need to know more about how the world works at a younger age. I introduced the same life lessons I share in this book to my only daughter when she was of discernible age. Seeing how she benefited from my stories, I decided to write this book so that other children may benefit from them too.

You can help your kids on this journey if you use the topics in this book to engage them in meaningful conversation, adding your own stories to the lessons.

Joseph Wong

PS: Throughout this book, I may write "he" or "she" but I could mean either.

I dedicate this book to my daughter

Amanda Jane Wong Xiu Wen

Prologue

Everyone wants to be a leader of some kind. It is invigorating and a sign of success.

But a leader doesn't need to be the one standing in front all the time. You can be part of a team and still be a leader.

My experience of leadership is that the more you work with people, make and correct your mistakes - this is most important - and learn from good leaders, the better a leader you become. So, if you're starting on the very first job in your life, my advice to you is to use the early stages of your work experiences to learn as much as you can - about decision making, people management and good leadership. Find a mentor (someone with experience and whom people look up to as a good leader), who would teach you these skills.

You see, although many qualities of good leaders can be taught, some qualities are either in you or not in you (either you're born with them or not). Qualities such as the wisdom to make the right decision in difficult situations and problem solving, require more than learning from others. This is why the sooner you understand how the world works, the sooner you learn to discover whether you possess these qualities, from the way you handle school, friendships and real-life situations.

If you have more questions after reading this book, you can write to me too.

Enjoy!

Joseph Wong

wojojo58@gmail.com

1

Be curious about everything!

D o you know how many chickens there are in the world?

Why is this relevant? Because one day, you may just need to use this information.

To be successful, you must be curious. Being curious means you want to know about as many things as possible. When you're always wondering and questioning - yes, even with things that don't matter to your job - you will be successful.

What's "always wondering and questioning"?

This means if you come across something new, find out how it works and why it is the way it is. For instance, if you come across a new word, go find out what it means, how to say it correctly and then find a way to use this new word - in a conversation or writing - within the next 48 hours. If you don't use it, you will forget. The more words you know, the more effectively you can communicate.

If I keep asking questions, won't people think I am stupid?

Actually, in my 36-year career, the people who asked questions were the most intelligent people in the room. Why? Because they were curious. They really wanted to know how things worked so that they could form their own opinions and make their own decisions about the matter. Don't think that asking questions is a sign of stupidity. If you are intelligent, people around you can tell from the way you think and behave. It is only when you don't know something and you don't ask, that you may look stupid when the time comes for you to talk about the topic.

A fact is true only for the moment!

Now, what do I mean by this? For a long time, everyone believed that the world was flat. It was only in 330 BC that Aristotle proved that the Earth is spherical in shape. And it was only in 2006 that the International Astronomical Union demoted the planet Pluto to a dwarf planet in our Solar System. So, you see, a fact may be relevant only for that moment. Stay curious and keep an open mind.

The internet today is full of lies and untruths!

That's true. So, how do you make sure you don't believe a lie? Here are some tips for you:

- DO NOT believe everything you read and hear on the news.

- CHECK the same facts from two other <u>reliable</u> news sources. Make sure the news sources are reliable and not someone's personal opinion.

- MENTION where you got the source of the fact if you are using the fact. Say something like "I read from Reuters News that...". Remember, the world is no longer flat and Pluto is not the ninth planet. A fact may be true only for the moment.

By the way, there are about 19 billion chickens in the world.

Something for you to think about

One good way to find out how things work is to ask "Why?" up to five times. Here's an example:

Lea   : You must boil the potatoes first.
Evelyn   : Why?
Lea   : You only have one hour. Potatoes need more time to cook.
Evelyn   : Why can't I just throw them on the grill?
Lea   : Because potatoes are starchy vegetables and need to be cooked all the way.
Evelyn   : Why can't I cook both the chicken and the potatoes on the grill?
Lea   : There isn't enough room on the grill for both items.

It is easy to learn how to do something and do it well. But it takes something special to know why we do those things and then make the right decisions if things go wrong. So, learn to understand how and why things work.

2

Let's talk about you

When you apply for a job at a company, you will usually need to send the company a document that talks about yourself - your name, age, address and a summary of your skills, abilities and accomplishments - so that they know a little bit about you. This document is called a résumé (pronounced 'rez-ziu-mei). Sometimes, they may ask for a curriculum vitae (usually just called CV) but the résumé is more widely used.

Remember that many people will be sending their résumés to the same company for the same job. Will they remember or notice your résumé? How do you talk about yourself so that you will stand out? Here are a few tips.

Tip Number 1: Say how useful you are to the company if they hire you

Even though your résumé talks about yourself, don't just say what skills you have, but how you can help this company do this job with your skills.

Say how you can help this company do this job with your skills.

Tip Number 2: Don't just use adjectives

Don't say you are "intelligent, hardworking, resourceful, creative..." Why? Because everyone else is saying the same thing. Look at these examples.

Here's a bad example:

"I received the Most Resourceful Team Member award in my final year innovations project".

Why is it a bad example? It does not say how good you are.

Here's a good example:

"In every project, I always find ways to achieve my objectives. In my final year innovations project, I did the following:

    a. Visited an actual paper factory in Jurong to learn the processes first hand

    b. Spoke with senior persons of three international paper companies to seek their views

    c. Video recorded these companies' own research results to substantiate our team's proposals

In so doing, I received the Most Resourceful Team Member award."

Tip Number 3: Put the more important skills first

When you watch an action movie, surely you want to see action as early in the movie as possible, right? It's the same with a company reading your résumé. Once you find out which of your skills are more important for this company, put them on page one. That means you want this company to read about these important qualities as early as possible.

How do you know what is more important for the company? Here are two ways.

- If this job needs someone to be quick and decisive, for example a project manager role, you must tell the company very early how decisive you are and how you always completed your assignments ahead of time.

- Research the company by visiting their website and read news about them in trusted news sites and magazines. From researching these, you will know what is important to the company.

For example, if they value volunteerism highly, you might want to list all your volunteer activities earlier in your résumé.

Tip Number 4: Keep your résumé short but powerful

Nobody likes to read a long résumé. It's worse if it is badly written. So, if you wish to make a positive impact, make sure:

- You use your words effectively.

- Your grammar is good.

- There are no spelling errors.

- You list down your more important skills as early as possible.

So, do you know what makes you so special?

Something for you to think about

Now that social media is available to everyone, remember that anyone can check up on what sort of person you are by looking at your social media page. That means the company you are applying a job at can also take a look at that page to check on you. Your social media page also becomes your public résumé. Therefore, be responsible when you write anything online.

3

Make someone like you in less than one minute

When you only have one minute to introduce yourself, can you make it memorable? Look at how these two boys talk about themselves.

Henry

Hi, I am Henry. I'm 11 years old and I study at Edgefield Primary School. My favourite subjects are Maths and Science. I love playing football. On weekends, when I am not playing football, I play computer games and go cycling around Punggol Park and Coney Island.

Darren

Hi, I am Darren. I'm 11 years old and I study at Edgefield Primary School. I love to find out how things work, so Maths and Science are my favourite subjects. I enjoy team sports such as football because I learn teamwork and leadership. On weekends, I keep my mind active with computer games and I love spotting otters and rare birds when I go cycling around Punggol Park and Coney Island.

Tell me - if you're picking someone to join your Science Quiz team, would you pick Henry or Darren?

I believe you'd pick Darren, right? Both Henry and Darren said identical things about themselves, yet we would remember Darren more than Henry. So, what made Darren more memorable?

Let's compare what they said side-by-side, shall we?

Henry	Darren
My favourite subjects are Maths and Science.	*I love to find out how things work, so Maths and Science are my favourite subjects.*

- By saying what his favourite subjects are, Henry merely states a fact.

- Darren, on the other hand, also states the fact that his favourite subjects are Maths and Science, but he also describes how he loves to find out how things work. Remember, earlier in this book, I said that being curious is a very good quality to have?

- If you want people to remember you, talk about the qualities that make you unique and not so much about what you do.

Henry	Darren
I love playing football.	*I enjoy team sports such as football because I learn teamwork and leadership.*

- Once again, Henry merely states the fact that he loves playing football.

- Darren says, in very few words, that he is a team player. He enjoys working in a team and he is learning to be a leader.

- If I am listening to Darren now, I am already thinking that I want him on my team.

Henry	Darren
On weekends, when I am not playing football, I play computer games and go cycling around Punggol Park and Coney Island.	*On weekends, I keep my mind active with computer games and I love spotting otters and rare birds when I go cycling around Punggol Park and Coney Island.*

- Some adults think playing computer games is a waste of time. So, by merely saying that he plays computer games on weekends, Henry could actually create a negative impression of himself.

- Although Darren says the same thing, he explains how he likes to challenge himself mentally with computer games.

- Darren shows again how curious he is as a person by talking about how he likes to spot otters and rare birds whenever he cycles outdoors. This statement also strengthens his claim that one of his favourite subjects is Science. I believe that Darren is an honest person too.

Do you wish to be more like Darren? Here are three tips to help you speak like him:

Tip Number 1: Know what would interest your audience

Nobody likes to hear an uninteresting story. So, make your story interesting. Do you know what your audience would be interested in? Not always, but you can make a clever guess. When you speak to a chef, talk about "food" in your conversation. When you speak to an elderly person, talk about "the good old days".

Tip Number 2: "So What?"

So what? It sounds rude to ask "so what?", doesn't it? But it's a useful tool to check if what you are saying would interest your audience. Look at this example.

You tell your football team to do warm up exercises before they start their game, but the lazy ones may not take your advice seriously. Let's ask "so what?" to this and say it again.

You   : "Do your warm up before the game."
      "So what?"

You   : "Do you know it is possible for your muscles to tear? Not only are torn muscles extremely painful, you may not be able to play football for a whole year! How do you prevent torn muscles? You must do a good warm-up before each game."

After explaining it this way, don't you think your team would be more interested to do a good warm up?

Tip Number 3: Prepare in advance

If you already know about an event, plan what you want to say ahead of time. The two key reasons are:

1. You know who your audience is, so you can prepare something that would interest them after asking "so what?".

2. If you have to talk about yourself in one minute, you know exactly what to focus on that would make your audience remember you.

In the adult world, there is something called the elevator pitch. Why is it called the elevator pitch? Imagine one day, you get to work and ride the elevator (lift) with the Chief Executive Officer (CEO) of the company you are working for. He is the Big Boss. He pays your salary. So, it's just the two of you in the elevator. He introduces himself to you and asks what you do in his company.

If it was Henry, he might simply say "I'm Henry. I work in Sales".

Let's see how my tips help you prepare in advance for this elevator pitch moment.

- **Tip Number 1: Know what would interest your audience**

  What would make the CEO happy? That his company made some money! So tell him about a deal that your team helped win, for example, "I work for Barry Chow in Sales and we were responsible for winning the recent autonomous vehicle deal."

- **Tip Number 2: "So what?"**

  If you just said "I am from Sales", the CEO might think "so what?". Saying your boss's name - Barry Chow - makes this conversation more real. Then you go on to say you were in the team that won a significant new deal that the CEO is happy about.

What those terms mean

Elevator pitch	"Pitch" here means your speech. Most elevators take 30 seconds to a minute to reach your respective floors. So, if you only have that time to impress someone, what would you say? A good elevator pitch is a well-prepared and well-rehearsed one. So, go work on your elevator pitch today for the unexpected moment when you have only a little time to make someone remember what an interesting person you are.

4

The big picture

Have you heard of the story of the three bricklayers?

Well, one day, while they were laying bricks, someone came along and asked them what they were doing. The first bricklayer answered, "I'm laying bricks". The second one said, "I'm putting up a wall." The third replied, "I'm building a cathedral".

Each bricklayer gave a different answer, but they were all correct. The difference lies in the way each of them regards his job. We all should learn from the third bricklayer. In any job or task we do, always see how our job leads to the ultimate goal. In the case of the three bricklayers, they were laying bricks to build a cathedral. The cathedral was the ultimate goal, not the wall.

When adults talk about the big picture, they mean understanding the purpose of something instead of just a small part.

Don't just perform a task, understand why we do what we do

When you eventually find work, the company may be so big that many of their processes are done by different people and maybe in different countries. Remember I said very early on that you must be curious? Let's use the example of the maker of Porsche cars. The Porsche factory may have the following teams:

- Design
- Inventory
- Electrical

- Interior

- Chassis

- Engine

- Assembly

- Painting

- Testing

If your job is to install the engine to the car, how do you describe what you do? If you are like the first bricklayer, you might say, "I install engines in cars." If you are like the second bricklayer, you might say, "I am doing step 6 of 9 steps in a car factory." And if you are the third bricklayer, your response might be, "I am building a Porsche." When you understand how you contribute to the ultimate goal, your job becomes more meaningful:

1. You see the value that your work brings to the company.

2. You understand why things are done that way and it makes you more curious about how the other processes work.

3. No matter how small a part you are doing now, being more responsible for what you do, serves as a motivation for you to become more successful in your job.

Getting to know more people is very important for your career

When you start to see the big picture in every task, you will need to connect with people from other parts of the company. This simple step of meeting and talking to them allows you to build your professional network. Networking is a powerful marketing tactic to help you become more successful in life. Earlier, we learned how to introduce and make yourself memorable for your audience. Apply those skills here when you start to meet people because someone may have a more interesting job for you.

Knowing the big picture helps you solve problems

When things go wrong, you can fix them more quickly if you understand how the entire process works.

Knowing the big picture also encourages greater cooperation between teams

When we know how all the steps are connected, we can encourage teams at every step of the process to help each other succeed. When everyone is focused on helping each other reach the ultimate goal, no one is competing to outdo the other. Everyone works towards the same goal.

This is especially useful for those new on a job. Don't say, "This is what my boss told me to do." If you wish to be successful, be like the third bricklayer and start learning everything there is to know about the job. You are, after all, building a cathedral.

What those terms mean

The big picture | When we "look at the big picture", we look again at what we are trying to achieve. Sometimes it is difficult to understand why we need to do certain things, but it becomes clearer when we remind ourselves what our ultimate goal is. For example, while planning an event, you realise you have to buy an additional item for $100. You know that you cannot spend any more money. But if you don't buy this item, the event might fail. Let's look at the big picture. How much would you be paid if the event was successful? $2,500. So, are you going to let $100 additional expense prevent you from earning $2,500?

Network | Imagine how convenient life is if you had a doctor, a reliable contractor, a trusted teacher or simply someone who's very good at fixing things, as friends? The more people we know, the easier it is for us to get things done. These people don't just appear in our life. We consciously make an effort to connect with them. And so they become part of our network. Having a big network is one of the most important things in your work life. Be careful not to make friends only because you want to use them. Everyone in a network benefits because they can share knowledge and connections.

Marketing | When we market something, we promote or advertise it. Remember, not everyone wants to buy what you are selling. But when more people know about it through good marketing, more people may want to buy from you.

5

To succeed, believe in yourself!

The popular Korean TV drama series Jewel in the Palace (released in 2003), set in the 16th century, is based upon the real life of Jang Geum, who started life in the Royal Palace as a kitchen help, but had a fascination for medicine and spent all her free time reading medical journals and experimenting with herbs. In one episode, the crown prince became paralysed after eating herbal duck stew and even the Royal Physician could not diagnose the cause. That did not stop Jang Geum from carrying out her own investigations. Her roommate told her to give up on her quest, saying, "If the Royal Physician can't find the cause, what hope do you have?"

Jang Geum continued to seek knowledge despite overwhelming odds and eventually became the first female Royal Physician in Korean history. Isn't that cool?

We must be respectful but we mustn't let it cripple us

Most of us who are brought up in an Asian culture are taught to embrace deference (pronounced 'def-rens') and respect. These are great virtues. But we mustn't think we are less worthy than others. When we go through life believing that we are not good enough, we often end up finding excuses to explain why we fail.

"Somebody with more experience is better than us." (deference)

"Somebody with higher education is more suitable than us." (respect)

If we continue to think this way, we will never be successful. To be successful, we must first believe in what we are really good at. Yes, there will be others who may be better than us in certain things.

But we, too, have qualities that make us better than them in other things. You cannot be better than everyone at everything. So, if you don't already know what your unique talents are, go and find out.

Talk to yourself!

Once you find out what your unique talents are, believe that you can use them well. One way to do this is to constantly talk to yourself when you are preparing to do something. Here are some examples:

1. Before you step up to make a speech before the whole school, say to yourself, "Everyone knows I am the best person to give this speech. I am confident I will do this very well."

2. Before you step onto the field to play against a powerful football team, say to yourself, "We have the skills and will power to win this game."

3. Before you do something for the first time in your life, say to yourself, "I am capable. I am so ready for this. I can do this!".

Look at these famous people who did not allow anything to stop them from achieving their goals:

-   Thomas Edison, the man who invented the light bulb, was told by his teachers in school that he was "too stupid to learn anything".

-   Albert Einstein, possibly the most famous genius in our lifetime, did not start speaking until he was four years old, and could not read until he was seven.

-   Steven Spielberg, the great American movie director, producer and screenwriter, was rejected by the University of Southern California's School of Cinematic Arts, not once, but TWICE!

-   Before Jack Ma founded Alibaba and became a billionaire, he was one of twenty-four applicants looking to work at Kentucky Fried Chicken. Twenty-three of the applicants got the job; Jack was the only one who did not.

We are in control of our own destiny

Which of these two advice do you like more:

"Manage your expectations
and you will manage
your disappointments."

"Whether you think
you can or you can't,
you're right."

Have you made your choice?

I will share my point of view and see if you agree with me, all right?

"Manage your expectations and you will manage your disappointments"

This advice is almost inviting failure. It goes back to the Asian values of deference and respect - that if we fail, there is a consolation prize. I'm not saying we would not fail or that we need not plan. When we do anything by focusing only on not being disappointed, we are focusing on the wrong target. We are, in fact, telling ourselves "We will fail and it's OK."

"Whether you think you can or you can't, you are right"

This famous advice comes from Henry Ford. It means if you think you can do it, you are right. It also means if you think you can't do it, you are also right. So, whether you succeed or fail, your mindset has a big part to play. Which do you choose to think? When you always think you can, you are more likely to be successful. Remember, we are in control of our own destiny.

So, what if we think we can, but we fail?

Yes, that could happen. Then you take the failure as a lesson to become better next time.

You want to be successful? Then know what your unique talents are and find the right environment to develop them. Don't just wish you could do something. A dream remains a dream until you do something with it.

What those terms mean

Deference   When you respect someone, you show respect to this person. In some cases, deference makes us submit to others because we believe that we are not good enough. While it is good to be respectful, we must also know when our talent and experience are needed.

6

What is a leader?

Who wants to be a leader?

ME! ME! ME!

It's great that you want to be a leader. The world needs more good leaders. So, what does it take to be a good leader? I share with you five qualities that make a good leader.

1. **Honest and real**

   A good leader must be honest. He does things for the right reasons and not to make himself popular. So, he is not an actor playing the "role" of a leader. Being a real leader means he is consistent with his decisions and people trust him to always make the right decisions. In life, not every decision is a happy one, so be prepared to accept the good and the bad, but be honest.

2. Committed to doing the best

A good leader accepts all challenges in his job. He is responsible for everything that he has to do because he is committed to his leadership. So he will be saying "Let's make this work!" and not "Just anyhow do it!". He does not give up, no matter how big the challenge is. When he is positive, he inspires confidence in his people too.

3. Calm and composed

A good leader does not shout and scream when things go wrong. He is focused on solving the problem first. Because he is confident of his and his people's abilities and knows what excellence looks like, a good leader knows that there is a solution for every problem and is creative in finding one.

4. Good communicator

A good leader is clear with what he wants. He understands what people want and ensures his message is clearly understood. Communication is two ways. So, being a good communicator also means he listens to the views and opinions of others.

5. A good leader creates new leaders

A good leader is not someone who sits on a throne and commands his people. A good leader takes the trouble to coach and develop his people into better individuals to not only help the team but also to improve on their careers. He is not afraid that someone would take over his job. When his team succeeds, it means he succeeds. A good leader is someone who creates new leaders from among his people.

7

When can you become a leader?

A ctually, the first day you report to work in your new job is the day you are being judged if you can be a leader one day.

How?

- By your work attitude.

- By how you treat your superiors and teammates.

- By the decisions you make.

You see, everything you say and do reveals a little more about yourself – how you react to a situation, how you manage a tight deadline, how you solve problems. Since good leaders make good decisions, your everyday behaviour at work reflects whether you make a good leader.

To help you behave like a leader at work, here are some simple but useful tips.

1. Never make a decision when you are angry

When you are angry, you are highly emotional. You would most likely make a decision based on how you feel at the time and because you are angry, this decision is likely to be illogical. So, never make a decision when you are angry.

2. Never make a decision when you are happy

When you are happy, you are also highly emotional. You may be so happy that you might promise more than you can deliver. For example, if your boss gave you a day-off for

21

doing a great job, but asked if you could work on a new but unfamiliar assignment, you might be so happy that you agreed even though you knew nothing about that topic. As it happened, you did a bad job of the unfamiliar assignment and upset your boss.

3. **Always use facts**

Trust evidence. A good leader bases his decisions on facts, not assumptions, guesses or rumours. When you can explain your decisions using verified facts and a logical conclusion, you get work done a lot faster and you are more respected and trusted.

4. **Take time out**

When you feel you are not ready to decide on something, take time out until you are reasonably calm to think logically. You can always say, "I need more time to think about this. I want to make sure we do the right thing."

5. **Keep your word**

Integrity means being honest and honourable. A good leader has integrity. If you told a customer that you would call back, make sure you call back. When you are known to be trustworthy, you will be given bigger responsibilities in your job, which will improve your chances of becoming a leader one day. Now do you understand why I said you must never make a decision when you are angry or when you are happy?

6. **Let your boss know how you are doing**

Your boss may not always notice your good work. Therefore, you will need to regularly update him on what you have done. When he knows more about the kind of person you are, it is easier for him to use your best talents. When updating your boss on what you have done, be careful not to turn this into a contest between you and your teammates to win over your boss. When you update your boss on what you have done, it is more about telling him what you have completed and what you intend to do next. It is also to check with him if you are doing the right thing and if there is anything else he wants you to do. This way, you are also seeking your boss's approval and advice.

A good leader takes control. You must show your boss and your teammates that you are mature enough to har dle any situation, especially when faced with a problem. Say something like, "Let's not panic. If we put our heads together, I'm sure we can find a solution." By always being positive, you also make people less nervous and put everyone in the right frame of mind to work on a solution.

8

Who is your customer?

When you get a job, who pays your salary?

Your boss?

Yes. And who pays your boss's salary?

The company?

Yes. And where does the company get its money from to pay your boss?

The customer. The people who buy from your company.

So, let me ask the question again - who pays your salary?

It's the customer.

The customer pays your salary.

Because if your customers don't buy, the company would not have money. If the company has no money, will your boss get paid? Will you get paid? No.

That's why I started this book by telling you to be curious. If the customer is so important - they pay your salary - you need to know more than what you do in your job. Imagine if each time your customer asks you a question, your answer is "I don't know"? Do you think the customer will be happy?

Here are some things you can do to make your customers happy.

1. **Know what your customers like**

   Find out what your customers like. Read about what customers like or listen to them. When they complain about your service or something they bought from you, don't just fix the problem or worse still, ignore them. Understand what they are complaining about and why. Then do something to make sure this problem does not happen again. Make them happy!

2. **Know what other companies are doing**

   Do you know the story of the frog in the well? From the bottom of the well, the frog only sees a bit of the sky and lots of the wall of the well. To this frog, this is his whole world. Isn't that sad? Believe it or not, some people are like this frog. Don't just focus on what you are doing. Do you know what other companies are doing? If your customers one day stop buying from your company and start buying from someone else, who is going to pay your salary? So, find out what other companies are doing to make their customers happy. Don't be afraid to learn from others about how you can do the same.

3. **Give your customers something nobody else can give**

   Do something special that your customers love so much and will continue to buy from you. Better still, do something that others cannot copy. Maybe it's great service, rewarding long-time customers with loyalty gifts or extending privileges to their family members.

Now that you know why it is important to treat your customers well, let me ask you this next question. Who is your customer? You have two choices.

☐ The external people who buy from your company.
☐ Your teammates and other colleagues in your company (even those overseas).

The answer is BOTH are!

Yes, the people in your team and everyone who works in your company are also your customers.

We call your teammates and colleagues in your company "internal customers" and the ones who buy from your company and pay your salary "external customers".

If your internal customers fail, or do something wrong, who suffers? The external customer. Yes, the ones that pay your salary. So, you must treat everyone in your company with genuine love and care just like you would external customers.

When you become a leader, you will face many challenges.

You will need to learn how to make the right decisions.

Look out for *I'm So Ready For Life Book 3*

to learn how to make decisions when things

are out of your control.

Printed in the United States
By Bookmasters